Social Media and Unfair Dismissal

Don't Tweet your way to a P45

CILINNIE NGO-PONDI

ISBN-13:
978-1508411963

ISBN-10:
1508411964

DISCLAIMER

No part of this publication may be reproduced or transmitted in any form or by any means, mechanical or electronic, including photocopying or recording, or by any information storage and retrieval system, or transmitted by email without permission in writing from the publisher.

While all attempts have been made to verify the information provided in this publication, neither the author nor the publisher assumes any responsibility for errors, omissions, or contrary interpretations of the subject matter herein.

The information provided within this book is for general informational purposes only. While we try to keep the information up-to-date and correct, there are no representations or warranties, express or implied, about the completeness, accuracy, reliability, suitability or availability with respect to the information, products, services, or related graphics contained in this book for any purpose. Any use of this information is at your own risk.

Adherence to all applicable laws and regulations, including international and local governing professional licensing, business practices, advertising, and all other aspects of doing business in the United Kingdom or any other jurisdiction is the sole responsibility of the purchaser or reader.

Neither the author nor the publisher assume any responsibility or liability whatsoever on behalf of the purchaser or reader of these materials.

Any perceived slight of any individual or organisation is purely unintentional.

TABLE OF CONTENTS

1 INTRODUCTION.. 1

    How to use this guide.. 2

2 SOCIAL MEDIA AND INTERNET USE MISTAKES 3

    2.1 Vicarious Liability 4

    2.2 Harassment and discrimination 4

        Discrimination by e-mail 5

        Harassment on Facebook... 5

    2.3 Breach of contract 7

    2.4 Implied duties.. 7

        The implied duty of mutual trust and confidence 7

        The implied duty regarding health and safety at work............... 7

    2.5 Cyber bullying, trolling and mobbing 8

        Protection from Harassment Act 1997 8

        Joint Enterprise... 9

        Malicious Communications Act 1988... 9

        Equality Act 2010 9

    2.6 The duty to obey reasonable and lawful orders 9

        Workplace policies.. 9

    2.7 The implied duty of good faith and fidelity.............................. 10

        Confidentiality.. 11

        Bringing the employer into disrepute 11

Copyright/Intellectual property 13

2.8 Restrictive Covenants 13

LinkedIn 14

Outlook 16

2.9 Privacy of posts 17

2.10 Defamation and Libel 21

2.11 Data Protection 22

2.12 Posts and emails can be used in evidence against you 25

2.13 Conduct outside of work 25

2.14 Bring your own device (BYOD) 27

Chapter Resources 27

3 DISCIPLINARY ACTION 29

3.1 Employers Duty to Act reasonably and follow a Fair Procedure 29

The Duty to Act Reasonably 30

The Reasonableness Test / Band of reasonable responses 31

The Duty to follow a Fair Procedure 31

The ACAS Code of Practice on Discipline & Grievance Procedures 32

Internal disciplinary policy and procedure 33

Chapter Resources 35

4 DEFENDING YOURSELF 36

4.1 Workplace Policies 36

4.2 Wrongly applied policy 37

4.3 No workplace policy...39

4.4 Unclear policy...41

4.5 Correctly applied policy...42

Chapter Resources..43

5 A DEFENCE BASED ON HUMAN RIGHTS...........................44

5.1 The Article 8 defence..45

5.2 The Article 10 defence..46

6 NO DAMAGE TO REPUTATION DEFENCE........................52

APPENDICES..58

Appendix 1 - Checklist...58

Appendix 2 – Statement of defence..60

EMPLOYEE RESCUE...63

ABOUT THE AUTHOR..64

Table of Cases

Benning v British Airways [2010] 20

British Home Stores v Burchell (1978) 32

Campbell v MGN [2004] 45

Crisp v Apple Retail UK Ltd.[2011], ... 11, 44

Edward RocknRoll v News Group Newspapers [2013] 45

Fairstar Heavy Transport NV v Adkins and anor 26

Fairstar Heavy Transport NV v Adkins and Another [2012], ... 26

Flexman v BG International Ltd [2011] 38

Gill v SAS Ground Services Ltd [2009], ... 26

Gosden v Lifeline Project [2009], ... 26

Gosden v Lifeline Project[2009]. 26

Hays Specialist Recruitment (Holdings) Ltd v Mark Ions [2008] 15

J Lerwill v Aston Villa Football Club Ltd.[2010] 40

Kass v Gillies and Mackay Ltd (unreported – July 2013) 56

Limpus v London General Omnibus [1862] 23

Lloyd v Grace Smith [1912] 22

Mason v Huddersflied Giants Rugby League FC (unreported – July 2013) 56

Novak v Phones 4U [2013] 6

Otomewo v The Carphone Warehouse Ltd [2011] 5

Pay v UK [2009] 46

PennWell Publishing (UK) Limited v Ornstein and others[2007] 16

Polkey v. A. E. Dayton Services Ltd [1988] 33

Preece v J D Wetherspoons plc [2011] 11

Smith v Trafford Housing Association [2012] 54

Smith v Trafford Housing Trust [2012]. 48

Taggart v Teletech UK Ltd [2011] 47

Taylor v Somerfield Stores [2007] 57

Teggart v TeleTech [2012] 17

Teggart v TeleTech [2012]. 17

The Law Society and Others v Rick Kordowski [2011] 24

Trasler v B&Q Ltd [2012]. 55

Trasler v B&Q Ltd ET/1200504/2012 55

University of Nottingham v Fishel [2000],ICR 1462 3

Walker v Charles Russell Solicitors [2007] 5

Walters v Asda Stores Ltd [2008] 42

Weeks v Everything Everywhere LtdET/2503016/2012, ... 54

Western Provident v Norwich Union Life Assurance [1997] 22

Whitham v Club 24 Ltd t/a VenturaET/1810462/10 53

Whitmar Publications Limited v Earth Island Limited [2013] 15

Young v Argos Ltd 57

For Nick, Aaron, Rhianna and Luke – my Four Reasons

1 INTRODUCTION

Social media is a way of using the internet to interact and share business as well as personal interests with other people all over the world. The 3 main networking sites that get people in trouble at work are Facebook, LinkedIn and Twitter, but there are others including Pinterest, Google +, YouTube, Instagram and many more. Facebook was 10 years old on 4th February 2014. 24 million people in Britain log on to Facebook every day[i]. As of 2014, LinkedIn had 15 million users in the UK[ii] as did Twitter. In addition to these main players there are various other platforms, blogs, forums and comment spaces on information websites. Suffice it to say that social media is huge and you are probably a user of one or more of these platforms. Together with emails and text messaging, the one thing they all have in common is that using them carelessly may cost you your job and worse.

You can Tweet and re-Tweet, post status updates, like, comment and share opinions and information instantly with a national and global audience. The problem is that once it's gone, it's gone! There are no safeguards, you don't know where that communication is going and unlike some e-mails, once you hit that button you have no way of recalling what you've sent. Even if you delete your account, the communication can be saved and shared.
It remains permanently in the ether to come back and haunt you, when you least expect it.

Using your personal social media account to share with "friends", "followers" and "connections" can still cause problems at work because you have no control over who they share your communication and personal information with. Misuse or inappropriate use of social media, email and text messaging can create criminal and civil liability for you and your employer. Most criminal offences that can be committed by using words or images can be committed using social media, and the legal repercussions are

1

the same as in off-line activity. There is no specific regulation of social media, so existing employment, criminal, data protection and human rights laws apply.

How to use this guide

The fact that you have used social media or the internet inappropriately will not always lead to dismissal if you use this Guide to thoroughly prepare your case and defence. In a worst case scenario, your preparation could give you enough ammunition to negotiate a settlement agreement and leave on agreed terms rather than be dismissed.

By using this Guide you will have the tools to understand and address the different problems that can arise with the Internet, E-mail, Social Media and other electronic communication tools and applications.

The Guide breaks down case law in a user friendly way so that you can easily apply cases to your particular situation.

The Guide is supplemented by information on the website – www.employeerescue.co.uk and covers everything you need to know, taking you quickly and simply through essential information on;

- Your legal rights
- Case law
- Remedies and compensation
- Templates
- The latest information on social media in employment

If it is alleged that you have breached your employer's policy on social media, it is likely that you will face disciplinary action, which could lead to disciplinary sanctions, including dismissal. You will have the opportunity to put your case forward at a disciplinary hearing. If your employer should dismiss you, you will have another opportunity to ask your employer to re-consider the decision at an appeal hearing. If the dismissal is confirmed, you can apply to ACAS for Early Conciliation if you believe that your dismissal was unfair. Employee Rescue has several Guides available on the website, www.employeerescue.co.uk to assist you in pursuing your chosen direction.

2 SOCIAL MEDIA AND INTERNET USE MISTAKES

Your actions at work are regulated by the terms of the employment contract and controlled by your employer. Anything you do that would normally be a breach of the employment contract, or a criminal offence, remains so if done on-line. In **University of Nottingham v Fishel [2000], ICR 1462,** the Court said;

"The employee's freedom of action is regulated by the contract, the scope of his powers is determined by the terms (express or implied) of the contract, and as a consequence the employer can exercise (or at least he can place himself in a position where he has the opportunity to exercise) considerable control over the employee's decision-making powers."

This means that your actions could be subject to the following repercussions for you as an employee and also for your employer;

For an employee

    i. Breaching a workplace policy - disciplinary action.
    ii. Criminal offence - criminal liability and disciplinary action
    iii. Tort - County Court or High Court Civil Liability

For an employer

    i. Employment Tribunal liability
    ii. Criminal offence - criminal liability
    iii. County Court or High Court Civil Liability
    iv. Health and Safety Executive action
    v. Information Commissioners Office action
    vi. Intellectual Property Office action

You can see from the above, why an employer would not take misuse or inappropriate use of social media, email and text messaging lightly. It can create criminal and civil liability for you and your employer. It would most definitely result in disciplinary action, possibly dismissal and in some instances legal action against you as an individual[iii].

2.1 Vicarious Liability

Your employer is responsible for anything you do in the course of employment so your employer could also be liable for your actions in Court. Vicarious liability or responsibility is when legal liability is imposed on an employer for the mistakes of its employees. Your employer is vicariously liable for what you do in the course of employment. This means that your employer is responsible for what you do during work hours, as well as what you outside_work hours if it impacts on work.

In most workplaces, you are permitted to access social media through your employer's facilities and sometimes via your own personal device. If you use your employer's IT equipment, mobile phone or server inappropriately during business hours or even in your own time, your employer could be vicariously liable for your actions.

2.2 Harassment and discrimination

The **Equalities Act 2010 (EqA 2010)** provides protection from discrimination and harassment in the workplace if you have a "protected characteristic". The protected characteristics are disability, gender reassignment, marriage and civil partnership, pregnancy and maternity, race, religion or belief, sex and sexual orientation[1].

EqA 2010 defines harassment as *"unwanted conduct related to a protected characteristic that has the purpose or effect of violating an individual's dignity, or creating an intimidating, hostile, degrading, humiliating or offensive environment for him or her"*[2].

Anything done by a person in the course of employment must be treated as also done by the employer[3]. This makes your employer vicariously liable if you harass or discriminate against a colleague or third party in the course of your employment. This applies even if your employer did not authorise your actions. Discrimination and harassment can happen on-line through e-mails and social media. If the bullying and harassment does not fall within **EqA 2010,** it will be covered by the **Health and Safety at Work (etc.) Act**

---

[1] www.employeerescue.co.uk/discrimination
[2] S26 EqA 2010
[3] S109 EqA 2010

1974 (HSWA 1974) as well as the **Protection from Harassment Act 1997 (PHA 1997).**

Discrimination by e-mail

Walker v Charles Russell Solicitors [2007] was the first discriminatory email case. Rachel Walker, a secretary with Charles Russell Solicitors who happened to be black, handed in her notice to the firm in 2001. The assistant solicitor Adam Dowdney e-mailed a partner, Clive Hopewell, asking, *"Can we go for a real fit busty blonde this time? She can't be any more trouble and at least it would provide some entertainment!!"* Mr. Hopewell replied; *"I was about to say the same!"*

Ms. Walker saw the e-mail and complained to the firm's head of personnel. Letters of apology followed from both Dowdney and Hopewell, but Ms. Walker took a case of sex and race discrimination to the employment tribunal. The claim was claim was settled out of the tribunal for an undisclosed sum. The Law Society took up the matter and launched an investigation through its Office for the Supervision of Solicitors (OSS). It was said that the OSS recommended that the Law Society reprimand the solicitors involved, including the senior partner of Charles Russell Solicitors for breaching its anti-discrimination rules and not taking appropriate investigatory or disciplinary action.

Harassment on Facebook

In **Otomewo v The Carphone Warehouse Ltd [2011]**, Mr. Otomewo was the manager of a Carphone Warehouse shop. He was suspended and investigated for alleged sexual harassment of a female colleague. When Mr. Otomewo returned from suspension, two members of his staff took his mobile phone without his permission while it was in the shop's back office. One of the employees used Mr. Otomewo's mobile phone to post a comment on the status update on his Facebook page saying: *"Finally came out the closet. I am gay and proud."* The employer subsequently dismissed Mr. Otomewo for breaches of the company's customer sales rules.

Mr. Otomewo sued the Carphone Warehouse for direct sex discrimination, direct sexual orientation discrimination and sexual orientation harassment. He won his claim for sexual orientation harassment on the basis that it was reasonable for him to be embarrassed and distressed by the status update, which was an unwanted and unnecessary intrusion into his private life.

As the comments were made during the course of employment the employer was vicariously liable for the conduct which amounted to harassment on the grounds of sexual orientation.

The employment tribunal later noted that Mr. Otomewo is not gay and did not believe that his colleagues thought that he is gay. The tribunal accepted that he was embarrassed and distressed by the change to his Facebook status because the comments were put on a public website that could be viewed by friends and family. The tribunal described the actions of his colleagues as an *"unnecessary and unwarranted intrusion into his private life on a public space"*.

Under **EqA 2010**, where it can be shown that there is a continuing course of discriminatory conduct, the time limit for a claim begins to run from the end of that course of conduct. In **Novak v Phones 4U [2013]**, Mr. Novak was a store manager for Phones 4U. He fell down stairs at work on 26th February 2010, and was on long term sick leave from that date.

- On 10th March 2010, an employee of Phones 4U posted a Facebook mock photo of himself lying at the bottom of the stairs in the same position that Mr Novak had landed after his fall.
- On 31st March 2010, another employee of Phones 4U, posted comments onto his Facebook page which made fun of Mr Novak's fall. Other employees of Phones 4U posted their "likes" of the comments.
- On 26th July 2010, a new Facebook post was made about Mr Novak's fall and his colleagues made further comments about the post.

Mr. Novak sued Phones 4U in the Employment Tribunal for race discrimination (because he was American), harassment and victimisation. He also said that his employer had failed to take such steps as were required by statute to stop what he regarded as discriminatory conduct. The Employment Tribunal dismissed certain parts of his claim as they were out of time. The Employment Tribunal said that although the 31st March posting was linked to the 10th March comments, it did not involve the same individuals, the subject matter was different and there was a break of 7 weeks between the 10th March and 26th July postings. Mr. Novak did not agree with the Employment Tribunal and appealed.

The Employment Appeal Tribunal (EAT) considered whether the claim was within the 3 month time limit, because of the gap between the Facebook postings, and ultimately agreed with Mr. Novak. The EAT said that comments made on Facebook over a period of 5 months were a continuing course of conduct for the purposes of the **EqA 2010**. The posts were linked by subject matter, people, and time.

2.3 Breach of contract

Breaching a workplace policy or rule would be a breach of contract. You also need to be aware that emails can form contractual documents. You must be absolutely careful of what you write in an e-mail, since once it's gone, it's gone! You can easily create a contract with an ill thought out e-mail, which then creates contractual obligations for your employer. If your employer is unable or unwilling to fulfil the terms of such a contract, then your employer could be liable for a breach of contract claim.

2.4 Implied duties

There are contractual terms that are implied into the employment contract. These have been developed by the courts (also known as the common law) and will be implied in circumstances where it is necessary to do so, or if the parties would have agreed to those terms after discussion[4]. Some of the relevant implied terms are;

The implied duty of mutual trust and confidence

The employment relationship is based on mutual trust and confidence. Your employer must not behave in a manner that is calculated or is likely to destroy or seriously damage that trust and confidence without a good reason (reasonable and proper cause)[5]. An example is where an employee is bullied or harassed through the internet, and the employer does nothing about it or does not do enough. This implied term applies to employees as well. Breach of a workplace policy would also be a breach of the implied duty of mutual trust and confidence.

The implied duty regarding health and safety at work

Every employer has a duty to take reasonable care of the health and safety of their employees. This is a common law as well as a statutory duty under HSWA **1974.**

Section 2 and 3 HSWA 1974 impose obligations on employers and the self-employed to ensure, as far as is reasonably practicable, the health and safety of their employees and members of the public who might be affected by their activities.

Your employer has a duty to protect all employees from bulling and harassment through social media, email and text messaging to ensure, 'so far as is reasonably practicable' the health, safety and welfare of their

---

[4] Lister v Romford Ice and Cold Storage Company Ltd. [1957]
[5] Woods v WM Car Services (Peterborough) [1982]

employees and to provide a suitable working environment. The duty includes taking reasonable steps to protect employees from unacceptable treatment.

This means;

- If you are bullied at work through social media, email and text messaging by a colleague or third party you could have an employment tribunal claim.
- If you bully a colleague through social media, email and text messaging you would face disciplinary action. Your employer is vicariously liable for what you do at work, and your employer could face an employment tribunal claim from your bullied colleague.
- If an employee has suffered psychiatric injury, that employee can make a personal injury claim in the County Court or High Court.

2.5 Cyber bullying, trolling and mobbing

Cyber bullying is using the internet, mobile phones, or other technology to send or post text or pictures intended to hurt or embarrass another person. Trolling is the intentional disruption of an online forum, by causing offence or starting an argument. There is also on-line mobbing, where a number of people will make comments to or about a person because they dislike that person's opinions.

Facebook pages, newspaper comment sections, twitter and other on-line forums are bombarded with insults and threats. Some people says it's just banter and argue their right to freedom of speech. If you carry out cyber bullying, trolling or mobbing in the course of employment to a colleague or a third party outside your workplace, it could cost you your job and your employer could be vicariously liable under the following provisions;

Protection from Harassment Act 1997
Under the **Protection from Harassment Act 1997(PHA 1997)** it is unlawful to "pursue a course of conduct" that the perpetrator knows, or ought to know would amount to harassment. Harassment is not defined in the **PHA 1997** but does include oppressive and unreasonable behaviour, calculated to cause alarm or distress. **S1 PHA 1997** creates two classes of criminal offence. The lesser offence is liable to summary conviction, whilst the offence of harassment can also be an offence under the **Police and Criminal Evidence Act 1984 S24 (2)**. **S3 PHA 1997** provides that any offence under **S1** may be the subject of a civil claim by the

affected person. The Act holds employers vicariously liable for the actions of employees in the course of employment. A person can bring a claim under this Act up to 6 years after the bullying rather than the 3 months allowed for unfair/constructive dismissal and under anti-discrimination law.

Joint Enterprise

There is a long-standing common law concept in criminal law of "joint enterprise", where several people can be charged with the same offence, even though they may have played very different roles in the crime. Joint enterprise can apply to all crimes, and so can be applied to offences under **PHA 1997**. This means that it is possible to be prosecuted for an offence in which the people involved did not know each other and acted at different times and in different places.

Malicious Communications Act 1988

Sending a communication which is grossly offensive and has the purpose of causing distress or anxiety is an offence under section 1 of the **Malicious Communications Act 1988.**

Equality Act 2010

If the cyber bullying is about a protected characteristic under **EqA 2010,** an employer could face a claim of unlawful discrimination, even if the target of the bullying does not have the protected characteristic.

2.6 The duty to obey reasonable and lawful orders

Every employee is bound by the duty to obey lawful and reasonable orders at work. The word lawful covers statutory laws provided by parliament as well as the employment contract. Workplace policies, memo's, notices and e-mails about workplace expectations and behaviour may form part of your contract.

Workplace policies

The contract of employment often includes the staff handbook and other workplace policies. A workplace policy can be an express term of your contract. Express terms are those which have been accepted by you and your employer as part of the contract. They may or may not be in writing. ACAS recommends that all employers should have a policy on internet and social media use[6].

Most employers have such a workplace policy covering internet and email use. These workplace policies generally state what you can and cannot do as far as internet, email and social media use. The policy should also state what will be regarded as gross misconduct by your employer. Even if your employer does not have such a policy in place, you could still get in trouble for gross misconduct if you misuse the internet and communication systems at work. Tribunal cases are lost by employees where the employer is able to prove that there was a breach of an existing workplace policy. The law allows you to refuse to act on an unlawful, unreasonable or dangerous instruction[7]. Your employer can dismiss you for refusing to follow a lawful and reasonable order even if it is not written in your employment contract or workplace policy.

Many professional regulators have social media policies specific to the particular profession, which is usually aligned to the professional code of conduct. A professional such as a nurse, doctor, accountant etc. would be expected to adhere to their particular regulators rules as well as those of their employer. Breach of the one can also be breach of the other, so you end up facing disciplinary proceedings with your employer as well as professional sanctions.

2.7 The implied duty of good faith and fidelity

Any action by an employee which seriously harms an employer's business is a breach of the implied duty of good faith and fidelity (loyalty). The duty applies during working hours and does not extend after termination of the contract of employment. Whistleblowing under the **Public Interest Disclosure Act 1998** is excluded from this implied duty.

This duty imposes an obligation not to work in competition with your employer. It also imposes a duty of confidentiality so that you must not disclose your employer's confidential information and trade secrets to third parties or use your employer's confidential information for your own purposes.

Confidential information can be information about other employees in the organisation, but could also extend to client confidentiality and intellectual property.

---

[6] ACAS: Social Media - http://www.acas.org.uk/index.aspx?articleid=3375
[7] Morrish v Henlys (Folkestone) [1973]

Any information that you post on a public forum about your employer's business can give rise to a breach of these duties.

Confidentiality

In the case of **Crisp v Apple Retail UK Ltd. [2011]**, Apple dismissed Mr. Crisp for posting several status updates on his Facebook account about Apple and its products from home, even though only his personal friends could see the comments. Mr. Crisp posted *"once again, f**k you very much work"*, openly criticised an Apple application and described an IPhone as a *"Jesus Phone"*. Mr. Crisp's last status update said "Tomorrow *is another day, a day I hope I will forget"*. He posted this the day before Apple released their new tagline "Tomorrow is another day, a day you'll never forget". Apple found out, and Mr. Crisp was dismissed.

Mr. Crisp sued Apple and lost his case. The Tribunal emphasised the fact that Mr. Crisp had received Apple's workplace policy which stated that employees should not do anything which might damage the company's image. Apple placed a lot of importance on its brand image, stating in its employee policies and training materials that protecting its image was a "core value", and had highlighted that making derogatory comments in social media would be treated as gross misconduct. Apple had also provided training about conduct outside of work, particularly behaviour on social networking sites. The Tribunal also said that Mr. Crisp had no control over his Facebook page, as he could not control whether his comments would be passed on or shared by others. Mr. Crisp was therefore in breach of Apples workplace policies which had been clearly explained to him, and as a result he had been fairly dismissed.

Bringing the employer into disrepute

Preece v J D Weatherspoon's plc [2011] had the same outcome. Miss K Preece was employed by J D Weatherspoon's as a Shift Manager until she was dismissed for gross misconduct for posting comments on Facebook during work hours.

Miss Preece and a colleague were working at the Ferry Boat Pub in Cheshire, when Miss Preece was subjected to verbal abuse and physical threats by a group of people, particularly customers known as Brian and Sandra, who were subsequently asked to leave.

Later that evening Miss Preece received several telephone calls at the pub from a person claiming to be Brian and Sandra's daughter, which included a threat in the first call to *"get your f'ing P45 ready because you're out of here"*. Miss Preece took to Facebook to vent her anger, posting, *and "f**k off, f**k off"* immediately after the calls were received and whilst she was on duty. Later she posted *"f**kin hag"*. When she got home, in response to comments from another Facebook friend she posted that she hoped *"her hip breaks"*. This led to a complaint to the customer services department from Sandra's daughter, who said that these very public comments were offensive, and that her mother had a hip replacement in the past.

Miss Preece was dismissed for;

— Failing to comply with the company email, internet and intranet policy, specifically blogging which was found to lower the reputation of the organisation.
— Bringing the company into disrepute.
— Committing acts outside of work which had an adverse bearing on her suitability for the job.

Miss Preece sued J D Weatherspoon's for unfair dismissal (and an extra claim for non-payment of a bonus as an unlawful deduction from wages claim). JD Weatherspoon's said that it had reasonable grounds to believe that Miss Preece had committed an act of gross misconduct; it had carried out as much investigation as was reasonable, and the sanction fell within the range of reasonable responses.

The Tribunal agreed with JD Weatherspoon's. It said that whatever Miss Preece's belief about the privacy of her communications they were in the public domain. Miss Preece argued that Article 10 of the European Convention on Human Rights gives her the right to freedom of expression and information, including the freedom to hold opinions, and to receive and impart information and ideas. The Tribunal did not agree with her and said that JD Weatherspoon's actions had been justified under Article 10 (2) because of the risk of damage to reputation. It was clear from the communications that Miss Preece was discussing work and specific customers who had been barred. The Tribunal found that Miss Preece had not been unfairly dismissed and her claim for unlawful deduction from wages was dismissed.

Copyright/Intellectual property

You must not act in a way that breaches the copyright or intellectual property of your employer or others. Counterfeiting and piracy are intellectual property (IP) crimes. Friends and colleagues may send you links to video sharing sites like Couch Tuner. If you download a movie from Couch Tuner or other sites like it, you are possibly committing an IP crime, or in legal speak committing an "infringement". "Infringement" is a legal term for an act that means breaking a law. Intellectual property rights are infringed when a product, creation or invention protected by intellectual properties are exploited, copied or used in any way, without having the permission of the person who owns those rights. Your employer could be liable for a fine of up to £50,000, and you could be subject to a fine and a prison sentence of up to 10 years. Counterfeiting and piracy also affects your employers IT infrastructure with viruses, Trojans and other malware which can aid identity theft, threaten system security and slow down IT networks. Infringement of a trademark or copyright can be both a criminal and civil offence.

You can commit such an offence by;
— selling or producing DVD's or fake branded goods to your colleagues and outside the office.
— using the work intranet to such products to your colleagues
— using company servers and equipment to download unlicensed software
— using unlicensed software on business computer systems

For more on IP Crime see the Intellectual Property Office publication; Intellectual Property Crime and Infringement.

2.8 Restrictive Covenants

Whilst employed the implied duty of fidelity means that you will not supply information or trade secrets to third parties, or otherwise work against your employer's interests. The duty does not extend after your employment has ended. There are no specific legal controls after employment has ended and employers try to manage this by using restrictive covenants in the employment contract.

A restrictive covenant is a section (clause) in an employment contract which says that an employee is not allowed to compete with a previous employer for a certain period after the employment contract has ended. It can also say that the employee cannot deal with any customers of the previous employer by using information gained during the previous employment.

The types of restrictive covenants generally used are;

Non-dealing clause
This prevents a person from dealing with former clients, customers or suppliers in any way.

Non-competition clause
This restricts a former employee from working in the same industry or similar employment with a competitor.

Non-solicitation clause
This stops soliciting (poaching) clients, customers or suppliers of the previous employer.

Non-poaching clause
Prevents employees from stealing their former colleagues.

The Courts will generally not support a restrictive covenant against an employee on the grounds that it is a restraint of trade and contrary to public policy. If the previous employer can prove that the restrictive covenant is important to protect legitimate business interests, and it extends only as far as is reasonably necessary to protect those interests then it will be upheld and enforced by the Courts.

LinkedIn
LinkedIn has brought its own special legal issues when the contract of employment ends. LinkedIn works by allowing you to create your own profile, post your CV on-line and create your "connection". Connections are a list of your business contacts, friends and family, you can then make connections with other LinkedIn users to build up a network of contacts. Problems arise when employees take their LinkedIn profiles and contacts to their new job, poach clients or use confidential information in their own or a competitors business.

Some employers have taken umbrage when an employee updates his status on Facebook or LinkedIn to let previous customers know that he is in a new job. Employers have not been able to do anything about this yet.

It can be a breach of the implied duty of confidence and fidelity if you use a list of your employer's contacts to create Facebook friends or LinkedIn connections. In **Hays Specialist Recruitment (Holdings) Ltd v Mark**

Ions [2008] Mark Ions worked for Hays for more than 6 years. Hays encouraged all employees to use LinkedIn. Three weeks before resigning from Hays, he set up his own recruitment company called Exclusive Human Resources Ltd.

There were no clauses in Mark Ions contract that stopped him from setting up a competing business after the end of the employment contract. The employment contract did have clauses that stopped him from using Hay's confidential information, including its client database, and poaching Hays' clients for a period of 6 months after contract ended.

Hays sued Mark Ions in the High Court to make him hand over the list of Hays clients that he had contacted after he left Hays. This is called an "order for disclosure". Once they got the list from him, Hays would use the list as evidence to sue Mr. Ions in a further court case for copying and keeping Hays' confidential information in breach of his employment contract. Mr. Ions argued that Hays encouraged employees to use LinkedIn, and that once a Hays' contact accepted his invitation to connect, then that contact was no longer confidential as they could be contacted by anyone in Mr. Ion's personal network.

The Court did not agree with Mr. Ions because he uploaded client data on his LinkedIn network to use in his own business. The Court ordered Mr. Ions to produce a list of all of his LinkedIn business contacts so that Hays could see how much confidential information he had transferred, and the extent to which he had breached the employment contract. Mr. Ions was also ordered to disclose all documents, including invoices and emails, which showed any use of the LinkedIn contacts and any business that he got from them.

In Whitmar Publications Limited v Gamage, Wright and Crawley [20130, Mr. Gamage and two colleagues set up a rival publishing company called Earth Island, 4 months before leaving Whitmar Publications at the end of January 2013. Whilst employed by Whitmar Publications, Susan Wright had been responsible for managing the company's LinkedIn account. Whitmar Publications sued the three ex-employees together with their company Earth Island, and asked for an injunction to protect the contents of its LinkedIn account which Whitmar Publications said was confidential information.

Whitmar Publications claimed that the ex-employees been actively competing against Whitmar before they even ended their employment. They had taken business cards and databases of its customers. Whitmar said that it used those LinkedIn groups to promote its business interests and that they had been maintained using its computers.

Susan Wright had refused to hand over the LinkedIn account password because she said they were her personal connections. Mr. Gamage agreed to return the business cards to Whitmar, but before doing so he used the Card Munch App to convert photographs of business cards directly into LinkedIn contacts.

Whitmar's Linked-In groups were used as the source of a group email inviting people an Earth Island launch event at a bar in Leicester Square. The terms and conditions of LinkedIn say that any information held in a LinkedIn account belongs to the account-holder, and there were no clauses stopping them from dealing with Whitmar's clients after the end of employment, but the Court supported Whitmar Publications and granted an injunction to stop Gamage, Wright and Crawley from using the LinkedIn account or the contacts on the business cards.

Outlook

Outlook or other database address lists created and contained on your employer's IT system belong to your employer and may not be copied or removed from the workplace. In **PennWell Publishing (UK) Limited v Ornstein and others [2007]** , the Court said that where an employee, who was a journalist, created and kept all his contacts on his employer's computer system that database or list of information belonged to the employer. This included personal contacts and business contacts which the employee had before joining the employer. If the employee had kept a separate list of contacts and selectively copied those which were his own contacts on to his own computer, he would have been able to use them.

Twitter

Are Twitter accounts and passwords company property or trade secrets? This is what was considered in the American case of **PhoneDog v Noah Kravitz [N.D. Cal. Nov. 8, 2011]**, PhoneDog is a mobile device news and reviews website that employed Noah Kravitz as a product reviewer and video blogger. Whilst working for PhoneDog, Noah Kravitz had 17,000 followers under the Twitter handle @Phonedog_Noah. He left the job in October 2010 and kept the same Twitter account, but changed his handle to @noahkravitz. In January 2011, he started working for Technobuffalo which is PhoneDog's competitor, using his Twitter account.

PhoneDog said that he took 17,000 of its Twitter followers with him, and estimated that each follower was worth $2.50, so they sued him for the money.

Noah Kravitz asked the court to dismiss the case because but the court refused to do so, saying that Twitter accounts and their passwords could constitute trade secrets and that an employee who does not give up an account could be guilty of misuse of a trade secret or "trade secret misappropriation."

2.9 Privacy of posts

If you make offensive comments on social media about a colleague or comments that make reference to your employer, an employment tribunal may decide that you have been fairly dismissed. It would be difficult to argue that your employer has violate your privacy because once you post something publicly it is no longer private.

This what a Northern Ireland industrial tribunal said in **Teggart v TeleTech [2012].** Mr. Teggart worked for TeleTech UK Ltd, which provides call-center services for a number of clients. His Facebook friends included some of his work colleagues. At home, Mr. Teggart posted a message on his Facebook page about a female colleague [A] saying; *"Quick question who in TeleTech has [A] not tried to fuck? She does get around!"* A number of people posted comments in response to this message. [A] was not Mr. Teggart's Facebook friend, but she heard about it from another work colleague and asked Mr. Teggart to remove it through his girlfriend. In response to this request, Mr. Teggart posted another comment on Facebook that said; *"[A] can go and suck donkey dick ... LOL."* Again, a number of individuals made comments.

Mr. Spence was not a TeleTech employee, but he knew both Mr. Teggart and [A]. Mr. Spence emailed the comments to TeleTech and suggested that they were in breach of company policy. Mr. Riddiough, TeleTech's service delivery manager, spoke to [A] who was upset and tearful. , but did not take a statement from her at the time. Mr. Teggart accepted that he had made the posts, and was suspended.

Mr. Teggart was invited to a disciplinary hearing to answer allegations of;

— Making inappropriate comments on Facebook on multiple occasions in relation to fellow employee [A] which could constitute bullying and harassment.

— Using TeleTech's name in association with these comments within a social media forum which could bring the company into disrepute.

When he received the disciplinary letter, Mr. Teggart took to

Facebook and commented that, while he was not going to apologise to [A] his, *"intention was not to upset her just take the piss a bit but seems as if she may have taken it a bit too seriously so he'd knock it on the head"*.

At the disciplinary hearing, Mr. Teggart's said that;

— he had not intended to offend A;

— he was entitled to make any comments that he wanted on his personal Facebook profile;

— the reference to "TeleTech" was an abbreviation for telecommunications or technical and not a reference to the company;

— he considered the matter to be "fun or a joke"; and

— he was under the influence of alcohol when he posted the Facebook comments.

He was dismissed for gross misconduct on the basis that he had made multiple postings on a social media site regarding a fellow employee, one of which made reference to TeleTech. The company stressed that it considered that Mr. Teggart had harassed [A] and, in mentioning TeleTech, had brought the company into disrepute. This was contrary to the company's disciplinary policy, which lists "bringing the company into serious disrepute" as an example of gross misconduct.

Mr. Teggart sued TeleTech for unfair dismissal in the Industrial Tribunal. He said that the internal investigation had been flawed and argued that the company's code of conduct did not cover action in employees' personal life or personal use of the internet. Mr. Teggart said that he was expressing his personal opinions which were not made on behalf of the company, neither was he using TeleTech equipment. He said that his comments had been inappropriately brought into the workplace by another person. Mr. Teggart also argued that TeleTech had violated his human rights, namely the rights to respect for his private life and freedom of expression, and the right to manifest his beliefs.

The industrial tribunal accepted that there were problems with the investigation stage, but went on to say that, where the factual matters that give rise to a charge are accepted by the person charged, usually the investigation need not be as extensive or detailed as would normally be expected.

Bringing the company into disrepute

The tribunal said that the approach of the disciplinary panel was seriously flawed. While it was reasonable for the panel to be unconvinced that Mr. Teggart was using "TeleTech" as an abbreviation for telecommunications or technical, it had not considered whether or not the company had been brought into "serious" disrepute, which is the wording used in its disciplinary policy. The tribunal also expressed concerns that the company had not taken any evidence from Mr. Spence, who had first alerted it to Mr. Teggart's Facebook comments.

Harassment

The tribunal found that the disciplinary panel's conclusion that Mr. Teggart had harassed [A] was reasonable. Mr. Teggart's unwanted Facebook comments clearly violated her dignity and were capable of creating a degrading and humiliating environment. The company had evidence that [A] was upset about these comments and did not want to come into work. The tribunal also found that harassment can be caused through comments made to others and not to the victim of the harassment. Mr. Teggart's comments were sent to a number of other employees within the workplace and were known about on the day that they were placed on Mr. Teggart's Facebook page.

Human Rights

The tribunal concluded that TeleTech had not violated Mr. Teggart's human rights. When he made the comments public on Facebook, he abandoned any right to have his comments treated as private and he could not seek to rely on the right to respect for private life (Article 8 European Convention on Human Rights). The tribunal said that the freedom to manifest your beliefs under **Article 9 European Convention on Human Rights** does not extend to a comment about the promiscuity of another person. **Article 9** is intended to refer to *"a philosophy, set of values, principles, or mores"* guiding an individual's conduct or behaviour. The right to freedom of expression in Article 10 carries the responsibility to exercise that right in a way that is necessary for the protection of the reputation and rights of others. It did not entitle Mr. Teggart to make comments that damaged the reputation or infringed the rights of [A].

The tribunal dismissed Mr. Teggart's claim for unfair dismissal.

In **Benning v British Airways [2010]** British Airways dismissed Bryan Benning for gross misconduct on the basis that he had breached its data protection, social media and bullying and harassment policies. Mr. Benning sued for unfair dismissal. At the hearing, the tribunal was told that Mr. Benning, writing under the pseudonym 'Strike 2010', made comments aimed at strike-breaking cabin crew and staff. He posted the comments in response to another YouTube writer, called 'Ruthless Interloper' who was later identified as being a BA pilot.

The messages said; *"All crew hate nigels - they are glorified bus drivers.*
'Cabin crew want nothing to do with you anymore. Enjoy your nights in your chinos, polo shirt and eating your chicken wings. We have a whole number of scab's details, and car details.
'By the way, don't eat anything you are to be served on board. Bring your own food on board. We know everything, we have all your details.'
The posts included abusive messages about other British Airways strike-breakers on YouTube, including sinister threats saying he knew *'car and other details of scabs.'*

As part of his defence, Mr. Benning said that he was suffering from a debilitating bout of severe depression and was not acting in the best way during his disciplinary hearings. He was advised by his doctor that he could not take part in the hearing and he could not answer questions over the phone. He was severely depressed, on pills and did not have a union representative. He also said that he was provoked into posting messages because of what other people had said, including one blogger writing under the name 'Powerful Peanuts'.

A video, which was shown to the panel, showed Powerful Peanuts saying:
'Cabin crew you are paid £30,000 a year and all you do it open a packet of dry roasted nuts and walk up and down an aeroplane; you have no qualifications or skills.
'The women are only employed if they have a nice ass and male cabin crew members have those faces you want to punch - and I would love to - until it looks like a beef burger.
'You are glorified waiters and waitresses. The hardest part of your job is putting ice cubes into tiny glasses.'

Mr. Benning, responded to this post by saying: *'You stupid tw*t.*
'Go cut your head lice ridden hair and get a job. Do yourself favour and start wearing some deodorant.

'Like usual - a stupid fecking student who thinks he knows everything but in fact knows feck all. Go die in a compost heap you piece of s***.
'Your day will come to you silly piece of s*** and who will stand up for you?
He allegedly added: *'You will die a SCAB. You will take that title to the grave. Every day it will eat away at you. You deserve it. Oh - by the way, good riddance.'*

Mr. Benning's defence did not help. The Tribunal found that his dismissal was fair.

2.10 Defamation and Libel

Under the **Defamation Act 2013**, a person who considers that their reputation has been, or may be harmed by statements made by others, can sue in the High Court for unlimited damages or to prevent the perpetrator from making those statements. It applies to any comments or opinions posted on social media sites, and company intranets.

Section 5 of the Defamation Act 2013 forces website operators to remove offensive comments or hand over the names and addresses of perpetrators to the authorities. (See the Government website for guidance on the Defamation Act 2013[8].) Section 5 does this by creating a defence for a website operator hosting user-generated content (such as Facebook or Twitter) when they are sued for statements posted on their website;

If the website operator can prove that it did not post the statement on the website, then they will not be liable. This is subject to the following provision;

The website operator is liable if the person suing has proof that;

— He could not identify the person who posted the statement and so could not sue that person.
— He complained about the post to the website operator, and the website operator did not respond in accordance with the procedure in the **Defamation (Operators of Websites) Regulations 2013.**
— The website operator acted with malice in relation to the posting of the statement

This means simply, that the website operator has to identify the person who posted the offensive comment. If they are not able to identify the person,

---

8

https://www.gov.uk/government/uploads/system/uploads/attachment_data/file/269138/defamation-guidance.pdf then they will be liable. If you make an anonymous offensive posting, an offended person can sue Facebook or Twitter or whatever on-line forum you posted on. They in turn have to find you and turn you over to the authorities or face the law suit themselves.

Your employer would also be vicariously liable for defamation if the posting was done in the course of employment.

Western Provident Association v Norwich Union Life Assurance [1997] was the first case of libel by e-mail. A Norwich Union employee sent an internal email suggesting that a rival company, Western Provident Association was being investigated by the Department of Trade and Industry and that Western Provident Association was close to insolvency. Western Provident obtained an order for the preservation and delivery of copies of the emails.

Norwich Union was vicariously liable for the defamatory comments of its employees. An employer will be vicariously liable for the actions of its employee where an employee is acting within the scope of employment. The employer will be liable even if the act was not authorised[9], not for the benefit of the employer or expressly forbidden[10].

Norwich Union had to pay Western Provident Association approximately £450,000 in an out-of-court settlement and gave a public apology. Although an e-mail can be deleted from the screen, a computer will store copies which can be recovered and some e-mail systems automatically print out messages for record retention. A court can order a company to produce emails if those emails are relevant to the case.

2.11 Data Protection

Obligations under the **Data Protection Act 1998 (DPA 1998)** fall upon the data controller. Your employer is a data controller and has to handle all data under the eight data protection principles[11]. The seventh data protection principle says;

Appropriate technical and organisational measures shall be taken against unauthorised or unlawful processing of personal data and against accidental loss or destruction of, or damage to, personal data.

---

[9] Lloyd v Grace Smith [1912]
[10] Limpus v London General Omnibus [1862]
[11] Data Protection Principles - https://ico.org.uk/for-organisations/guide-to-data-protection/data-protection-principles/

This means that your employer as the data controller, must have appropriate security to prevent personal data from being accidentally or deliberately compromised. Your employer must;

— design and organise IT security to fit the nature of the personal data held, and the harm that may result from a security breach;
— be clear about who is responsible for ensuring information security in the company;
— make to have the right physical and technical security, backed up by robust policies and procedures and reliable, well-trained staff; and
— be ready to respond to any breach of security swiftly and effectively.

If you mishandle personal data at work such that there is an information security breach, or download software or malware that allows viruses and Trojans on your employer's IT system, you will most likely be disciplined. Your employer would also be liable under **DPA 1998.**

S36 DPA 1998 says that personal data processed by an individual for their own personal purposes is exempt from the data protection principles[12]. So if you are processing data for your own personal use, then you are not a data controller for the purposes of the act.

The Information Commissioners Office is clear that businesses or organisations that use social media do not fall within the exemption and continue to have responsibilities under **DPA 1998**. This is still the case even if an organisation gets a member of its staff to do the processing for it through their personal networking page. Posting information about people on social media can breach data protection laws[13].

In the case of **The Law Society and Others v Rick Kordowski (Solicitors from Hell case) [2011],** Rick Kordowski had a personal website called "Solicitors from hell".
The website allowed and encouraged people to anonymously post reviews and negative comments about solicitors and other legal professionals.
Mr. Kordowski moderated posts and charged a fee for adding or removing them. In November 2010 the Law Society made a complaint about Mr. Kordowski to the Information Commissioner. They said that Mr.

---

[12] employeerescue.co.uk/privacyatwork

Kordowski was a data controller, and he was not complying with the DPA. In January 2011 the Information Commissioner wrote to the Law Society explaining that he had decided not to take any action against Mr. Kordowski because **S36 DPA 1998** comes from **Article 10 European Convention on Human Rights (freedom of expression)** and allowed him to process data for his personal, family or household affairs.

The Information Commissioner said that **S36** is intended to balance the individual's right to respect for his or her private life with the freedom of expression. *"These rights are equally important and I am strongly of the view that it is not the purpose of the **DPA** to regulate an individual's right to freedom of expression – even where the individual uses a third party website, rather than his own facilities, to exercise this."*

The Law Society was unhappy with this, and sued for an injunction to close down "Solicitors from hell". In the High Court, the Judge did not agree with the Information Commissioner about how **S36** applied in this case.
Justice Tugendhat said that the first data protection principle states that personal data shall be processed fairly and lawfully. He said that if processing breaches the general law of confidentiality, then it would not have been processed lawfully and so it would be a breach of **DPA 1998**.
S32 DPA 1998 makes data that is processed for journalism, literature and art exempt. The Judge said that "Solicitors from hell" was not journalism, literature or art, and that it was against the public interest.

"Journalism that is protected by S32 involves communication of information or ideas to the public at large and in the public interest. Today anyone with access to the internet can engage in journalism at no cost. If what the Defendant (Mr. Kordowski) communicated to the public at large had the necessary public interest, he could invoke the protection for journalism and Art 10 of the European Convention on Human Rights. But for reasons given in many judgments in the cases against him referred to in this judgment, he cannot make any such claim, nor any claim at all for the protection under Art 10 for what he has communicated, because what he does is against the public interest. It has equally been established many times that the Defendant is responsible in law for what he communicates through the Website."

The Court said that Mr. Kordowski was a data controller because he moderated the site and charged a fee for posting or removing posts so he had to comply with **DPA 1998**.

With regard to the other data protection principles, he was in breach of;
— The First Data Protection Principle: **Personal data must be processed 'fairly and lawfully' and, in particular, shall not be**

processed unless at least one of the conditions in Schedule 2 is met. The word "lawfully" applies to any form of conduct that is unlawful, including breach of confidence, libel and harassment.

— The Fourth Data Protection Principle: **Personal data shall be accurate and, where necessary, kept up to date.**

— The Sixth Data Protection Principle: **Personal data shall be processed in accordance with the rights of data subjects under DPA 1998.**

The Court granted a permanent injunction closing down the website. Mr. Kordowski also had to block, erase and destroy all the data that was the subject of the case.

2.12 Posts and emails can be used in evidence against you

Employers can use evidence found on social media sites as evidence of misconduct.

In the case of **Gill v SAS Ground Services Ltd [2009],** Ms. Gill was a Customer Services Representative for SAS Ground Services. She was on full pay whilst on long-term sick leave and posted Facebook updates describing her choreographing and auditioning activities at London Fashion Week. SAS Ground Services found out and dismissed her. The tribunal agreed with her dismissal because her behaviour in claiming to be unfit for work was clearly dishonest.

In **Fairstar Heavy Transport NV v Adkins and Another [2012]**, the Court of Appeal said that Fairstar Heavy Transport was entitled to inspect and copy the business-related e-mails sent and received by its former Chief Executive Officer while acting on its behalf.

The company had the right to demand any documents about its business, including materials held and stored on a computer because there was an agency relationship between Fairstar and Mr. Adkins, which remained even after the employment relationship had ended.

2.13 Conduct outside of work

You can be dismissed for conduct outside work. Any postings, emails or text messaging that;

— can be linked to your employer

— is damaging to your employer
— has an impact on your ability to do your job
— causes offence to other employees

can cause you to face disciplinary action at work and possibly lose your job.

In **Gosden v Lifeline Project [2009],** Mr. Gosden was employed by Lifeline Project Limited, a charity that assisted drug users in prisons. HM Prison Service (HMPS) was one of Lifeline Project's largest clients and Mr. Gosden worked at Moorland prison. Mr. Gosden was disciplined by the governor of Moorland prison for his attendance, given a written warning, and banned from working at Moorland. He was then transferred to Lindholm prison.

Mr. Gosden sent an offensive sexist and racist email from his home computer outside working hours and from his home computer to the home computer of Mr. Yates, a colleague employed by HMPS. The email was a chain email which signed off with the sentence "It is your duty to pass this on." Mr. Yates forwarded the email to another colleague at the workplace and the email entered the computer systems of HMPS.

HMPS investigated this and Mr. Gosden was excluded from all HMPS prisons in Yorkshire and Humberside. As a result, Lifeline Project suspended Mr. Gosden and after carrying out an investigation found him guilty of damaging the company's reputation with HMPS and dismissed him for gross misconduct.

Mr. Gosden lost his employment tribunal claim for unfair dismissal. The tribunal said that it was within the range of reasonable responses for Lifeline Project to regard forwarding the email to an employee of one of its biggest clients as something which might damage its reputation or integrity.

The tribunal considered the impact of **Article 8 of the Human Rights Act 1998** which provides that "everyone has the right to respect for his private and family life, his home and his correspondence" and discussed whether it would be appropriate to dismiss for conduct outside the workplace. In this regard, it acknowledged that Mr. Gosden had, in his own time, from his home computer, sent an email to a friend's home computer.
The tribunal noted that if the email had been a piece of private correspondence written by Mr. Gosden and intended for the eyes of Mr. Yates only, it might well have found that privacy attached to it.

It stated, however, that the email had been prepared expressly with the intention that it would be passed on by its recipients, as it stated: 'It is your duty to pass this on'. The tribunal said that because of this it was not a confidential communication.

Mr. Gosden would have been aware that those to whom he sent it were likely to pass it on, and Mr. Gosden had no control over the persons to whom it might be passed.

2.14 Bring your own device (BYOD)

Your employer may supply you with a smart phone, laptop, tablet or USB devices, or allow you to use your own device for work. These all raise data protection issues. The Information Commissioners Office (ICO) guidance on Bring your own device (BYOD) explains some of the risks under the **DPA 1998,** as well as other concerns when personal devices are used at work.

The Employment Practices Code also published by the ICO offers clear guidance on the obligations of employers and employees on the separation of personal and corporate data to ensure compliance with **DPA 1998.**

Chapter Resources

ACAS

Social Media - http://www.acas.org.uk/index.aspx?articleid=3375

Social Media, Discipline and Grievances - http://www.acas.org.uk/index.aspx?articleid=3378

Social Media and Managing Performance - http://www.acas.org.uk/index.aspx?articleid=3376

Social Media and Bullying - http://www.acas.org.uk/index.aspx?articleid=3379

Social Media, Defamation, Data Protection and Privacy - http://www.acas.org.uk/index.aspx?articleid=3380

THE INFORMATION COMMISSIONERS OFFICE

Social Networking and online forms, when does the DPA apply?
- https://ico.org.uk/media/for-the-public/documents/1445/social-networking-and-online-forums-dpa-guidance.pdf

Bring your own device - https://ico.org.uk/for-organisations/guide-to-data-protection/principle-7-security/

The Employment Practices Code -
http://ico.org.uk/for_organisations/guidance_index/~/media/documents/library/Data_Protection/Detailed_specialist_guides/the_employment_practices_code.ashx

INTELLECTUAL PROPERTY OFFICE

Intellectual property crime and infringement -
https://www.gov.uk/intellectual-property-crime-and-infringement

3 DISCIPLINARY ACTION

In Social media and internet use dismissals, the decided cases show that the exact details of how the posting is made are not as important as whether the posting made a clear connection to a particular workplace.

Your employer is still required to follow the law, ACAS Code of Practice on Disciplinary and Grievance Procedures, and your employer's own policies and procedures.

The ACAS Code of Practice says that in any disciplinary situation,

— *Employers should raise and deal with issues promptly and should not unreasonably delay meetings, decisions or confirmation of those decisions.*

— *Employers and employees should act consistently.*

— *Employers should carry out any necessary investigations, to establish the facts of the case.*

— *Employers should inform employees of the basis of the problem and give them an opportunity to put their case in response before any decisions are made.*

— *Employers should allow employees to be accompanied at any formal disciplinary or grievance meeting.*

— *Employers should allow an employee to appeal against any formal decision made.*

3.1 Employers Duty to Act reasonably and follow a Fair Procedure

An employer unfairly dismisses an employee where he *"dismisses an employee without good reason or without following a fair procedure"*.

Section 98(1) Employment Rights Act 1996 (ERA 1996), says that in determining whether or not the dismissal of an employee is fair or an unfair, the employer has to show that the reason for the dismissal falls under one of the reasons listed in **S98(2) ERA 1996.**

Once the behaviour is deemed to fall into one of these two categories, the second question is whether the response of the employer in dismissing was a reasonable one under S98 (4) ERA 1996.

The Duty to Act Reasonably

The duty to act reasonably is a legal duty laid out in Section 98 (4) of the Employment Rights Act 1996. It says that the duty to be reasonable should be decided in accordance with equity and the substantial merits of the case. **Equity** means natural justice, procedural fairness, an employee's personal circumstances, common sense and common fairness. **Substantial merits** means "whether *an employee's behaviour or performance warranted dismissal*".

The Employment Tribunal will not consider whether you were actually guilty of the misconduct, but whether your employer believed and had reasonable grounds for believing that you were guilty of the misconduct at the time the decision was made. The only way that your employer can prove that they believed and had reasonable grounds for this belief is by proving that they acted within S98(4) ERA 1996.

Reasons for dismissal

First the Reason has to fall within the categories in **S98 (2)** ERA 1996 which provides five potentially fair reasons for dismissal. These are;

    i. Your lack of capability or qualifications to your job.
    ii. Gross Misconduct or repeated Misconduct.
    iii. Redundancy.
    iv. A legal bar or requirement which means that you cannot do the job.
    v. Some other substantial reason.

The potentially fair reasons which generally apply in such situations are for;

Gross misconduct or repeated misconduct[14]
Some other substantial reason[15]

---

[14] S98(2)(b) ERA 1996

Some other substantial reason applies where;
— The conduct has a significant impact on your relationship with your employer, work colleagues or customers;
— The matter brings, or could bring, the organisation into disrepute;
— The nature of the conduct makes you unsuitable for the type of work being carried out.

The Reasonableness Test / Band of reasonable responses

Second, your employer has to satisfy the "Reasonableness Test" in **S98 (4) ERA 1996.**

The Burchell Test

The duty to act reasonably was explained in the case of **British Home Stores v Burchell (1978)**. Where there is a dismissal, the court said that an employer must prove that at the time of the dismissal they believed that the employee was guilty of misconduct, that the belief was based on reasonable grounds and at the time of the belief they had carried out a reasonable investigation. In addition, for social media and internet use dismissals, your employer must prove that there was actual damage or the potential for damage to its reputation or business as a result of the posting.

The Balance of Probabilities

This means that it is up to your employer to prove that you have a case to answer. This task of proving or disproving is commonly described as "the burden of proof". The Burden of proof is decided on "the balance of probabilities" The balance of probabilities means that something is more likely than not to have occurred, or it is more likely than not that the incident did not occur. If the probabilities are equally balanced then your employer has not satisfied the burden of proof.

The Duty to follow a Fair Procedure

The requirements of a fair procedure are laid out in case law, the ACAS Code of Practice on Discipline & Grievance Procedures, your employment contract (or collective agreement) and your employer's internal disciplinary procedure.

The Duty to be reasonable and the Duty to follow a fair procedure go hand in hand. They both have to be satisfied.

---

[15] S98(1)(b) ERA 1996

The Polkey Principle
In the case of Polkey v. A. E. Dayton Services Ltd [1988], The House of Lords said that procedural fairness was an integral part of the statutory test for reasonableness, and a dismissal could be unfair purely because an employer did not follow fair procedures. This means that even if the employer was reasonable under S98 (4) ERA 1996, but breached the duty to follow a fair procedure, then the dismissal will be unfair.

The Polkey Reduction
If your employer was reasonable under S98 (4) ERA 1996 but did not use a fair procedure, the Employment Tribunal will reduce your compensation because you would have been dismissed if fair procedures had been followed.

The ACAS Code of Practice on Discipline & Grievance Procedures
ACAS says that social media misconduct should be treated in the same way as any other misconduct.

— The Code applies to all disciplinary action except redundancy or the non-renewal of fixed term contracts when they expire. Your employer does not legally have to follow the Code, but if they don't the Employment Tribunal will take this into account and increase your compensation by up to 25%. They can also reduce compensation by up to 25% if they believe that you have unreasonably failed to follow the Code.

— It sets out the basic principles that should be followed by your employer in any disciplinary procedure. If your employer does not have a policy on discipline, you can refer to the ACAS Guide on Discipline and Grievance at Work which complements the ACAS Code of Practice 1 – Disciplinary and Grievance Procedures. Even if your employer has a policy make sure that it is within the ACAS code and guidelines.

— Whenever a disciplinary process is being followed it is important that your employer deals with issues fairly. This means that;

> *Employers and employees should raise and deal with issues promptly and should not unreasonably delay meetings, decisions or confirmation of those decisions.*

> *Employers and employees should act consistently.*

> *Employers should carry out any necessary investigations, to establish the facts of the case.*

Employers should inform employees of the basis of the problem and give them an opportunity to put their case in response before any decisions are made.

Employers should allow employees to be accompanied at any formal disciplinary or grievance meeting.

Employers should allow an employee to appeal against any formal decision made.

— The Code also covers how people who are ill or disabled are treated when dismissed by their Employer because of their incapacity.

Internal disciplinary policy and procedure

Generally, in cases where the employment tribunal has decided that a dismissal for inappropriate internet use was fair the employer has had a clear social media and internet use policy in place. You need to check your privacy settings, and **THINK BEFORE YOU TYPE**.

The disciplinary procedure must contain the following processes in accordance with rules of natural justice. ACAS defines natural justice as the basic fundamental principles of fair treatment. These principles include the duty to give someone a fair hearing; the duty to ensure that the matter is decided by someone who is impartial; and the duty to allow an appeal against a decision. If your employer's procedure misses any of these elements it will be unfair and your employer will be liable in the Employment Tribunal.

  i. An Investigation – To establish the facts of the case
 ii. Notify you of the problem – Through a notice of disciplinary action
iii. Disciplinary Hearing – To give you an opportunity to respond
 iv. Representation – Your right to be accompanied at the disciplinary hearing
  v. Disciplinary Sanctions – It is only after completing the above that your employer can decide on appropriate disciplinary action
 vi. Appeal – After the appropriate disciplinary action has been decided you must be given an opportunity to appeal the decision.

Your employer is required by law to outline the disciplinary rules and procedures in the written statement of the terms and conditions of your employment within 2 months of the start of your employment. This is known as a **Section 1 statement**. **S3 (1) ERA 1996** says that the Section 1 Statement must include the disciplinary rules and procedure which apply to your employment.

> *"(1) A statement under section 1 shall include a note—*
>
> *(a) Specifying any disciplinary rules applicable to the employee or referring the employee to the provisions of a document specifying such rules which is reasonably accessible to the employee,*
>
> *Specifying any procedure applicable to the taking of disciplinary decisions relating to the employee, or to a decision to dismiss the employee, or referring the employee to the provisions of a document specifying such a procedure which is reasonably accessible to the employee,*
>
> *(b) Specifying (by description or otherwise)—*
>
> *(i) A person to whom the employee can apply if dissatisfied with any disciplinary decision relating to him or any decision to dismiss him, and*
>
> *(ii) A person to whom the employee can apply for the purpose of seeking redress of any grievance relating to his employment, and the manner in which any such application should be made, and*
>
> *(c)where there are further steps consequent on any such application, explaining those steps or referring to the provisions of a document explaining them which is reasonably accessible to the employee."*

The written statement can refer you onto your employer's full, written Disciplinary Policy, and make reference to a Social Media and Internet use policy or equivalent.

Your employer's disciplinary procedure must comply with the ACAS Code on disciplinary and grievance procedures as a minimum requirement. Some employers have separate procedures depending on whether the issue is one of conduct or performance. Disciplinary procedures should be clearly described in the disciplinary policy or your employment contract. They set out the standards of conduct that are expected and the sanctions that may follow if those standards are breached.

Anything that your employer discusses with you in relation to discipline will be kept on your personnel file and should be strictly confidential.

Chapter Resources

ACAS

Code of Practice on Discipline & Grievance Procedures -
http://www.acas.org.uk/dgcode2009

EMPLOYEE RESCUE www.employeerescue.co.uk

Facing Disciplinary Action -
http://www.employeerescue.co.uk/advice/i-dont-want-to-lose-my-job/im-facing-disciplinary-action/

4 DEFENDING YOURSELF

The fact that you have used social media or the internet inappropriately will not always lead to dismissal if you thoroughly prepare your case and defence. In a worst case scenario, your preparation could give you enough ammunition to negotiate a settlement agreement and leave on agreed terms rather than be dismissed.

Go to www.employeerescue.co.uk and use the resources on **Facing disciplinary action, Investigation, Your right to be accompanied, Suspension** and **Dismissal**.

Go through the outcomes of decided cases discussed throughout this guide, and particularly in this chapter. The decided cases show the points that an employer must consider in unfair dismissal coming under social media or internet use which are used in the Checklist at Appendix 1 of this guide.

Use the Checklist[16] to prepare your statement of defence[17]. Guidance on preparing your statement of defence is provided at Appendix 2 of this guide.

4.1 Workplace Policies

Your employer must have a social media policy in addition to the disciplinary policy. You stand a better chance of defending yourself, if there is no social media policy that states that your specific actions could be grounds for dismissal or if your employer applies policy incorrectly.

Get copies of the disciplinary, grievance and social media policies , go

---

[16] Appendix 1
[17] Appendix 2

through them and make sure that the allegations against you and how your employer will act on them are mentioned it. Make sure that your employer acts according to the policy and procedure. If not use the grievance procedure. If your employer has no policy, an unclear policy or misapplies policy you will have an employment tribunal claim for constructive unfair dismissal or unfair dismissal.

4.2 *Wrongly applied policy*

If your employer applies the existing policy wrongly, they would be liable in the employment tribunal. Use the checklist in Appendix 1 to ensure that the policy has been applied correctly to you.

Flexman v BG International Ltd [2011] was a case heard at the Reading Employment Tribunal about poorly handled disciplinary action against an employee for allegedly posting confidential information about company losses on his LinkedIn profile.

Mr. Flexman was employed by BG International as a HR Executive. He uploaded his CV on LinkedIn and ticked a box indicating that he was interested in "career opportunities". One of his colleagues anonymously reported him because his profile contained details of the company's "attrition rates". Mr. Flaxman's line manager asked him to take the offending material off LinkedIn as soon as possible. Mr. Flexman was on holiday at the time, and initially refused. After taking advice from friends and colleagues, he agreed to remove the material.

On his return from Mr. Flexman was informed of disciplinary proceedings against him on the basis that his actions amounted to a breach of their social media standards, a breach of confidence and a conflict of interest.

The Disciplinary Hearing
The disciplinary hearing was held on 21st April 2012. Mr. Goldader, the chair of the disciplinary hearing, said that Mr. Flexman should be given a slap on the wrist, but he would wait on his decision until he knew exactly what the nature of the confidential information was. HR then told Mr. Flexman that they did not have enough material to make a decision and they would need to meet again on 28th April 2012. Mr. Flexman queried this approach since he felt that it was not in accordance with the company's disciplinary process.

Mr. Goldader had said that he just needed further information on the confidential information in order to make his decision, but it appeared that

Ms. Raven, the adviser dealing with the case was also involved in the decision making process. Miss Raven then informed Mr. Flexman that that they would start the entire disciplinary process again with a new chair and HR adviser.

The Grievance
Mr. Flexman then brought a grievance against BGI International on 6th May 2011 about the decision to restart the disciplinary proceedings, rather than conclude the matter on 28th April 2011. At the grievance meeting on 20th May 2011 another manager Mr. Turnbull, was supported by Ms. Fox from the HR department. Mr. Turnbull said that they should go back to the disciplinary hearing, and review the way in which the legal and HR departments had handled the case. However, the company's legal representatives advised Mr. Turnbull that, before arriving at an outcome on the grievance, it would be more appropriate to conduct an investigation into the decision to restart the disciplinary process.

On 24th May 2011, Mr. Turnbull informed Mr. Flexman that he could not continue the grievance without further investigation. Mr. Turnbull's proposal to review the HR and legal departments' handling of the case was dropped. A grievance outcome meeting was eventually held on 9th June 2011. Mr. Flexman was informed that the original disciplinary process would continue with the original chair, but with different HR and legal representatives supporting him.

The Employment Tribunal Hearing
Mr. Flexman chose not to appeal the outcome of the grievance hearing. He resigned on 17 June 2011 and sued BGI International in the employment tribunal. He claimed constructive dismissal for making a protected disclosure and said that he had been subjected to a detriment for making the protected disclosure.

The tribunal said that from the time of the disciplinary hearing until his resignation, Mr. Flexman continued to believe that he was at risk of dismissal. The matter could have been more easily dealt with by an assurance to Mr. Flexman that the use of the phrase "our decision" in an email of 26 April 2011 did not mean that anyone other than Mr. Goldader was making the decision. Mr. Flexman had made it clear that he would be content for Mr. Goldader to confirm that the decision would be his own.

The tribunal felt that it was inappropriate for Ms. Raven to make the decision to restart the disciplinary process. She should have had no role to play in advising the manager making the decision. Ms. Raven knew where

Mr. Goldader stood, and it was wrong for the legal department to interfere with the decision of the chair.

The tribunal said that the way in which Mr. Flexman's disciplinary and grievance proceedings had been handled, particularly the delays, amounted to a breach of the employer's obligation of trust and confidence. Mr. Flexman had resigned as a direct result of the loss of trust and confidence in the employer to deal with the disciplinary and grievance proceedings. Mr. Flexman won his constructive dismissal claim.

What does this mean for you?

— Posting confidential company information on a social media website will lead to disciplinary action.
— You must remove the offending information when asked to do so.
— The information must be confidential and sensitive to justify disciplinary action.
— Your employer must use the policy and procedure correctly and in a way that does not cause you detriment.
— If your employer acts in a way that causes you detriment, you can resign and claim constructive dismissal for breach of the implied duty of mutual trust and confidence in the employment relationship.
— Your employer must take account of all the surrounding circumstances before deciding to dismiss.
— If you are unhappy with the process, raise a grievance.

4.3 No workplace policy

In **J Lerwill v Aston Villa Football Club Ltd. [2010]** there was no social media policy in place. Mr. Lerwill was Aston Villa FC's historian he had been an Aston Villa supporter for over 60 years. He had his own unofficial website about the club, and regularly contributed to fan forums. He had also written a published history of the club, called Villa Chronicles. In early 2009, Mr. Lerwill posted an article on an unofficial fan forum about a recent club match that he had attended. As a result of the article his line manager, Mr. Preece, asked him not to make postings on websites other than of a historical nature.

Mr. Lerwill was not given a formal warning and no disciplinary proceedings took place. On Christmas Day 2009, Mr. Lerwill was nursing his wife, who was unwell. To pass the time, he logged on to an unofficial fanzine forum, where he saw criticisms of an article that the posters assumed that he had written. In fact, the article had been posted by the club's media team, who had extracted it from an interview that Mr. Lerwill had given for the club's television channel. The criticism of the article worried Mr. Lerwill, who feared that the disparaging comments would affect sales of his book Villa Chronicles. Mr. Lerwill posted comments stating that he had not written the article and also made some other comments.

The Disciplinary Hearing

Aston Villa decided to take disciplinary action against Mr. Lerwill for making inappropriate and unprofessional comments towards fans in his capacity as a club employee, being critical of colleagues within the media team on a public forum, and posting comments on the message board despite being asked not to do so in early 2009.

At the disciplinary hearing, Mr. Lerwill said that he had been acting as an individual and not as a club employee, the inappropriate statements he made were because he was under a lot of stress at the time, he did not use bad language or criticise anyone directly by name and ultimately had done no harm to the club. He also said that he had been given any clear guidance about third-party communications and that the outcome of the exchanges on the forum had ended very positively. Aston Villa were not swayed by his arguments at the hearing or an appeal and dismissed Mr. Lerwill for gross misconduct.

The Employment Tribunal Hearing

Mr. Lerwill sued Aston Villa for unfair dismissal in the employment tribunal. Aston Villa referred to a clause in his job description requiring him to *"establish and maintain favourable contacts with the general public"*.

The tribunal accepted that the club had a genuine belief in Mr. Lerwill's misconduct and that there had been a reasonable investigation. However, the decision to dismiss fell outside the band of reasonable responses because Mr. Lerwill had not been told the severity with which the club would view his breach and there was no guidance in any policy or procedure or the employment contract that comments on a public message board could result in disciplinary proceedings and dismissal.

Aston Villa made a lot of the fact that everyone knew that Mr. Lerwill was its employee and any postings that he made would be seen as Aston Villa's own opinion. The tribunal did not agree with this since Mr. Lerwill was not aware that the club held this opinion. The employment tribunal agreed with Mr. Lerwill that he had been unfairly dismissed.

What does this mean for you?

— Your employer must have a social media and internet use policy.

— Your employer must make you aware of the policy and provide guidance on it so that you are aware of your obligations. Remember that if you are in a regulated profession, there may be professional rules even if there are no specific rules in the workplace.

— Your employer has to act fairly when it comes to previous warnings. Aston Villa said that the discussion between Mr Preece and Mr Lerwill in early 2009 was an informal warning. The tribunal said that it was unclear when it escalated from an informal chat to a management instruction, so that Mr Lerwill did not know that he faced dismissal for breaching the informal warning.

4.4 Unclear policy

In **Walters v ASDA Stores Ltd [2008]**, the policy was unclear. ASDA employed an external company to monitor blog sites where comments are posted about ASDA. The company did not have a policy on Social Media and internet use until 2008, when they published policy entitled "Internet abuse – don't blog your way into trouble!" The policy gave examples of misconduct on the internet. There were examples of "conduct-minor breaches", and "gross misconduct".

Ms. Walters had worked for ASDA for 10 years and was a Customer Services Manager for ASDA when this issue happened. A message was posted on Ms. Walters Facebook page which said, "*I work as a csm in Sutton ASDA all though I started off in sunny Skelmersdale on the rotisserie and even though im supposed to love our customers hitting them in the back of the head with a pic axe would make me feel far more happier heheh*".

<u>The Disciplinary Hearing and Appeal</u>
ASDA was notified by the external company and decided to take disciplinary action against Ms. Walters for bringing ASDA's name into disrepute with an act so serious that ASDA could no longer have trust in her as a Customer services Manager. In her defence, Ms. Walter said she did not post the message. The internet and email provider was AOL. She said she had lost control of her AOL account and her Facebook page, and that a hacker had posted the statements. AOL gave Ms. Walters a letter confirming that her account had been hacked and Facebook would not provide information without a court order. Ms. Walters also reported the hacking to the police.

ASDA did not believe Ms. Walters and summarily dismissed her for gross misconduct. At the internal appeal, Ms. Walters repeated her previous arguments. In addition she said that ASDA were inconsistent in how they applied their policy and gave printouts from a blog site called *"I work in ASDA and know I'm not always Happy to Help"*

She gave examples of several entries by existing staff, who had not been dismissed. In particular, she referred to an entry by a Ms. Wilson which said, *"That pissing bell that they have in the bakery. You get stupid customers ring it to get our attention and come and serve them. Im thinking id like to serve you that cold end of that bell and stick it as far up your arse as it will go. Whose bright idea was that???"*.

ASDA said one of the staff had been summarily dismissed, the other entries were not as serious as hers and said nothing about Ms. Wilsons post. Ms. Walter's summary dismissal was confirmed.

The Employment Tribunal Hearing
Ms. Walters sued ASDA for unfair dismissal and wrongful dismissal. The tribunal said that the decision to dismiss Ms. Walters was unreasonable because by their own policy, making the Facebook entry was misconduct but not gross-misconduct. ASDA was not entitled to summarily dismiss Ms. Walters, and her dismissal was unfair.

What does this mean for you?
— If there is a policy, have you received training on the potential disciplinary consequences of posting material online? Including training on protecting your employer's brand and the potential impact of your conduct outside work?
— Has the policy been applied fairly, or has it been applied differently to you?
  Dismissal must be a reasonable response so check if the comments fall into "gross misconduct" in your employer's policy, and whether the investigation was done fairly and in accordance with policy.

4.5 Correctly applied policy

In **Crisp v Apple Retail UK Ltd. [2011],** there was a policy which had been applied correctly, and employees had received training on the policy. Apple dismissed Mr. Crisp for posting several status updates on his Facebook account about Apple and its products from home, even though only his personal friends could see the comments.

Mr. Crisp sued Apple and lost his case. The Tribunal said that Apple had given detailed training on protecting its brand, which included exercising caution when posting online. Its email and electronic communications guidelines also stated that inappropriate use may result in disciplinary action.

What does this mean for you?
— Your employer must have a social media and internet use policy that must be clearly communicated to you.
— Your employer must provide guidance on the policy including what will be regarded as gross misconduct and the repercussions for employees. The policy must include details of;
> Permitted personal internet use
> What can be regarded as defamatory statements and consequences?
> Protecting your employer's reputation.

Chapter Resources

EMPLOYEE RESCUE – www.employeerescue.co.uk

The Disciplinary Hearing -
http://www.employeerescue.co.uk/advice/i-dont-want-to-lose-my-job/disciplinary-hearing/

Investigation - http://www.employeerescue.co.uk/advice/i-dont-want-to-lose-my-job/investigation/

Suspension - http://www.employeerescue.co.uk/advice/i-dont-want-to-lose-my-job/suspension/

5 A DEFENCE BASED ON HUMAN RIGHTS

If you are employed in the public sector, you may be able to argue that disciplinary action for your comment or statement is in breach of **Article 8** (the right to privacy) and **Article 10** (the right to freedom of expression) of the **European Convention of Human Rights**. The law has developed to provide privacy rights against both the state and private individuals through the tort of misuse of confidential information[18]. This means that the right to privacy can be applied to almost any form of social media activity, including posting photographs[19].

Even if you don't work in the public sector, under **S3** of the **Human Rights Act 1998 (HRA 1998),** employment tribunals must read and give effect to UK legislation in a way which is compatible with the rights laid down in the European Convention. This means that in deciding whether a dismissal is fair under **s98 ERA 1996**, employment tribunals have to interpret the section in a manner that is consistent with your convention rights.

This is not easy to achieve because the rights in **Article 8** and **Article 10** are "qualified rights". This means that the employment tribunal has to consider other matters in addition to your rights.

Article 8 – Right to respect for private and family life

"1. Everyone has the right to respect for his private and family life, his home and his correspondence.

2. There shall be no interference by a public authority with the exercise of this right except

---

[18] Campbell v MGN [2004

[19] Edward RocknRoll v News Group Newspapers [2013].

such as is in accordance with the law and is necessary in a democratic society in the interests of national security, public safety or the economic well-being of the country, for the prevention of disorder or crime, for the protection of health or morals, or for the protection of the rights and freedoms of others."

5.1 The Article 8 defence

The right to privacy is a fundamental right, protected under **Article 8** of the **European Convention on Human Rights** and **Article 7** of the **Charter of Fundamental Rights.** The law allows interference in this right where necessary in the interests of wider society.

Material posted on Facebook, even if you have set your privacy settings to private, will not be seen as private. It would be very difficult to win this argument in an employment tribunal.

In **Crisp v Apple Retail UK Ltd** for example, the employment tribunal considered the right to respect for private and family life under **Article 8.** The tribunal said that although Mr. Crisps Facebook page was "private", the nature of Facebook and the Internet means that a person's comments can very easily be forwarded onto others. Mr. Crisp had no control over how his comments would be shared and so he could not expect his posts to be private.

In **Pay v UK [2009],** Mr. Pay was a probation officer, employed by the Lancashire Probation Service since 1983. Following a tip off from the police in 2000, the Probation Servicer found out that in his leisure time Mr. Pay performed shows in hedonist and fetish clubs and was also a director of a company selling products connected with bondage and sadomasochism on the Internet. There were images of him and semi-naked women and men available online. Although Mr. Pay was well respected in his work for the probation service, his employer considered that his off-duty conduct was incompatible with his professional duties, particularly because he worked with sex offenders. Mr. Pay refused to stop these activities and was dismissed. Mr. Pay sued his employer for unfair dismissal, claiming that it violated his Article 8 rights. The European Court of Human Rights said that, while his right to privacy and freedom of expression had been interfered with, his dismissal was justified because of the nature of his work. His case was dismissed.

In **Teggart v Teletech UK Ltd [2011]** Mr. Teggart posted comments on his Facebook account outside of work about a female colleague's alleged promiscuity. When he was dismissed, he claimed unfair dismissal and that his right to privacy, freedom of expression and freedom to assert his beliefs had been breached., Mr. Taggart was unsuccessful in his argument that his Facebook comments about a female colleague's promiscuity was a private matter and his human rights had been breached.

The Tribunal said that he had harassed the woman, and his comments were in the public domain. He couldn't now argue that those comments were private. *"When the Claimant put his comments on his Facebook page, to which members of the public could have access, he abandoned any right to consider his comments private."*

This same rationale was applied in Gosden. Mr. Gosden used his personal email account to forward a sexist and racist chain email to another employee's personal email. The email ended with "IT IS YOUR DUTY TO PASS THIS ON". The other employee sent it to a third employee's work email address. The employer found the email on its system, saw that it had been initially sent by Mr. Gosden and dismissed him. The tribunal said that the dismissal was justified because the encouragement to pass the email on meant it was not a purely personal communication.

In **Preece v JD Weatherspoon's**, Ms. Preece was unable to use the Article 8 argument because she had 646 Facebook friends.

5.2 The Article 10 defence

Article 10 of the **European Convention on Human Rights** says that everyone has the right to freedom of expression and that that right may only be qualified in narrowly limited circumstances. Those circumstances include national security, public safety, the protection of morals, and the protection of the reputation or rights of others. You can argue that restrictions on your use of social media infringe your right to freedom of expression.

"Freedom of expression constitutes one of the essential foundations of a democratic society … It is applicable not only to 'information' or 'ideas' that are favourably received or regarded as inoffensive or as a matter of indifference, but also as to those that offend, shock or disturb …[20]"

Article 10—Freedom of expression

---

[20] Sunday Times v UK (No 2) [1992]

1. *Everyone has the right to freedom of expression. This right shall include freedom to hold opinions and to receive and impart information and ideas without interference by public authority and regardless of frontiers. This article shall not prevent States from requiring the licensing of broadcasting, television or cinema enterprises.*

2. *The exercise of these freedoms, since it carries with it duties and responsibilities, may be subject to such formalities, conditions, restrictions or penalties as are prescribed by law and are necessary in a democratic society, in the interests of national security, territorial integrity or public safety, for the prevention of disorder or crime, for the protection of health or morals, for the protection of the reputation or rights of others, for preventing the disclosure of information received in confidence, or for maintaining the authority and impartiality of the judiciary.*

Lord Bingham of Cornhill said *"There can be no yardstick of gross offensiveness otherwise than by the application of reasonably enlightened, but not perfectionist, contemporary standards to the particular message sent in its particular context. The test is whether a message is couched in terms liable to cause gross offence to those to whom it relates."*[21]

In **Teggart v TeleTech UK Limited**, the tribunal said that the protection in **Article 9** to express one's own beliefs was intended to protect your own "philosophy, set of values, principles or mores", and does not allow comments about another person's sexual activity and Article 10 will not provide protection if it infringes on another person's rights or reputation.

This means that you can only use the **Article 10** defence if your comment is lawful and does not state untruths about another person. This applies even if your comment upsets people with different views.

The **Article 10** right was considered in **Smith v Trafford Housing Trust [2012].** Mr. Smith worked as a Housing Manager for Trafford House Trust which is a non-political, non-denominational organisation.

Mr. Smith is a Christian. He had 201 Facebook friends most of who were fellow Christians.

45 of his Facebook friends were fellow employees of the Trust. He read a news article on a BBC news website headed: 'Gay church "marriages" set to get the go ahead'. Thinking the article might interest some of his Christian friends, he posted a link on his Facebook wall together with the heading *'an equality too far'*. Under this he posted, *"I don't understand why people who have no*

---

[21] DPP v Collins [2006]

faith and don't believe in Christ would want to get hitched in church the bible is quite specific that marriage is for men and women if the state wants to offer civil marriage to same sex then that is up to the state; but the state shouldn't impose its rules on places of faith and conscience."

Following comments from others, he posted;
".......I don't understand why people who have no faith and don't believe in Christ would want to get hitched in church the bible is quite specific that marriage is for men and women if the state wants to offer civil marriage to same sex then that is up to the state; but the state shouldn't impose its rules on places of faith and conscience."

These comments upset one of his work colleagues who also happened to be his Facebook friend. This friend reported Mr. Smith to their employer. Trafford Housing Trust included gay people among its clients, and took disciplinary action against him on the basis of;
— Posting comments on Facebook that had the potential to cause offence.
— Posting comments that could be seriously prejudicial to the reputation of the Trust.
— Serious breach of the Code of Conduct and the Equal Opportunities Policy.
— Failing to take managerial responsibility.

Disciplinary Hearing and Appeal
The outcome of the disciplinary hearing and internal appeal was that Mr. Smith was demoted to a non-managerial position with the Trust, with a 40 per cent reduction in pay. Mr. Smith continued to work in the more junior non-managerial role but sued Trafford Housing Trust in the High Court. His claim was that it was a breach of contract for the Trust to demote him and substantially to reduce his pay, when he was not guilty of any misconduct.

The Court Hearing
Two sections of the Trusts code of conduct were in issue. The first was headed "Relationships with Board members, customers, their friends and relatives, members of the public and with colleagues". Under that heading the following three passages were relied on by the Trust;

*"Employees are required to maintain the highest standards of personal/professional conduct and integrity at all times and to be courteous and considerate with all customers, their family and friends, colleagues and members of the public.
Employees are required to act in a non-confrontational, non-judgmental manner with all*

48

customers, with their family/friends and colleagues. The Trust is a non-political, non-denominational organisation and employees should not attempt to promote their political or religious views. Employees are expected to respect the customs and culture of any customers, their friends and family and colleagues.

Customers, their friends and family and colleagues must always be treated with dignity and respect."

The second heading was "Behaviour to external authorities/outside interests". The following passage was relied on by the Trust;

"Employees should not engage in any activities which may bring the Trust into disrepute, either at work or outside work. This includes not engaging in any unruly or unlawful conduct where you are or can be identified as an employee, making derogatory comment about the Trust, its customers, clients or partners or services, in person, in writing or via any web-based media such as a personal blog, Facebook, YouTube or other such site."

The Trusts argument in court were that;

— By identifying himself on his Facebook wall as a manager of the Trust, Mr Smith had created a real risk that readers of his two postings about gay marriage in church would think that he was expressing views on the Trust's behalf. This had the potential on undermining the Trust's determination to maintain neutrality on contentious matters of religious belief and politics.

— The expression of views by a manager which could cause distress to other employees or even customers could bring the Trust into disrepute, even if those people did not believe that Mr Smith was speaking on behalf of the Trust.

The court did not agree with Trafford Housing Trust. On point A, the Court did not consider that any reasonable reader of Mr. Smith's Facebook wall page could rationally conclude that his two postings about gay marriage in church were made on the Trust's behalf. This was because Mr. Smith's brief mention at the top of the page that he was employed as a manager by the Trust could not possibly lead a reasonable reader to think that his wall page consisted of, or even included, statements made on his employer's behalf. Secondly, it was obvious that Mr. Smith used Facebook for personal and social rather than work related purposes. The other entries made on the same page during that period related to sport, food, motorcycles and cars, none of which had any relevance to his work and all of which were about his personal and social life. His postings about gay marriage in church were not work related.

With regard to point B, the Court did not see how Mr. Smith's postings could bring the Trust into disrepute. It said that since the Trust prides itself on encouraging diversity both among its customers and its employees, it should accept that the encouragement of diversity in the recruitment of employees involves employing people with widely different religious and political beliefs and views, some of which may cause distress among the holders of deeply felt opposite views.

The Court could not envisage how his moderate expression of his particular views about gay marriage in church, on his personal Facebook wall at a weekend out of working hours, could sensibly lead any reasonable reader to think the worst of the Trust for having employed him as a manager.

The Court said that the right of individuals to freedom of expression and freedom of belief, taken together, means that they are in general entitled to promote their religious or political beliefs, providing they do so lawfully.
The Trust's argument was that since 45 of Mr. Smith's Facebook friends were fellow employees of the Trust this created a work related context to his use of his Facebook pages. He was therefore prohibited from promoting his religious or political views under the Code of Conduct.

Again, the Court did not agree because Mr. Smith's Facebook wall was inherently non-work related. Even though he stated that he was a manager at the Trust, he used his Facebook wall to express his personal views about matters which had nothing to do with his work. His Facebook was an aspect of his social life outside work, just like a pub, a club, a sports ground or any other place where people meet and chat.

Secondly, although Mr. Smith's Facebook wall was not purely private, he did not use it to force his opinions on his work colleagues. His Facebook wall was a virtual meeting place where those who knew of him, whether work colleagues or not, could attend at their own choice to find out what he had to say about a diverse range of non-work related subjects.

Finally, the critical difference between a targeted email and Mr. Smith's Facebook is that it was his colleagues' choice, rather than his, to become his friends.

Mr. Smith was free to express his religious and political views on Facebook, provided he acted lawfully.

"The frank but lawful expression of religious or political views may frequently cause a degree of upset, and even offence, to those with deeply held contrary views, even where none

is intended by the speaker. This is a necessary price to be paid for freedom of speech. To construe this provision as having application to every situation outside work where an employee comes into contact with one or more work colleagues would be to impose a fetter on the employee's freedom of speech in circumstances beyond those to which a reasonable reader of the Cod and Policy would think they applied. On any view their main application is to circumstances where the employee is working for the Trust. For the reasons already given, Mr. Smith's use of his Facebook involved his work colleagues only to the extent that they sought his views by becoming his Facebook friends, and that did not detract to any significant extent from the essentially personal and social nature of his use of it as a medium for communication."

The Court said that action taken against him was unlawful. The Trust did not have a right to demote Mr. Smith because of his Facebook postings. The demotion was a breach of contract by the Trust.

What does this mean for you?

— In such a situation you are better of arguing Article 10, than Article 8.

— Article 10 provides that everyone has a right to freedom of expression which can only be restricted in certain circumstances. One of which is for "the protection of the reputation or rights of others". If your comment does not impact on the rights of others then action taken against you will be unlawful.

— A tribunal or court will consider whether your comments were private.

— A brief mention of the identity of your employer or your position at work does not make your Facebook work related.

— Your employer can restrict or prohibit social media at work, or in a work related context, but cannot extend that prohibition to your personal or social life through a code of conduct or other workplace policy.

6 NO DAMAGE TO REPUTATION DEFENCE

It is not enough for your employer to argue that the social media policy has been breached. The legal test is that any damage or potential damage must be real and not merely fanciful. An employment tribunal will look at all the circumstances of the case in deciding whether your employer acted reasonably.

One of the factors the tribunal will consider is whether any harm was caused to your employer's business by the comments. In **Whitham v Club 24 Ltd t/a Ventura [2010].** Mrs. Whitham worked as a team leader at Club 24 Limited which provides customer services for the Volkswagen group. Mrs. Whitham posted a status update on Facebook which said, *"I think I work in a nursery and I do not mean working with plants."* In response to a post from a colleague she posted, *"Don't worry, takes a lot for the bastards to grind me down."* A former employee of Club 24 then posted, *"Ya, work with a lot of planks though,"* to which Mrs. Whitham replied, *"2 true."* She had about 50 Facebook friends and had set her privacy settings so that only they could see her comments.

Two of her Facebook friends who were also work colleagues reported her to the line manager and Mrs. Whitham was dismissed. Club 24 Limited said that her comments had put its reputation at risk and could have harmed its relationship with Volkswagen. The employment tribunal did not agree with Club 24. It said that the comments were mild, and that dismissing Mrs. Witham fell outside the band of reasonable responses. Mrs. Whitham did not mention Volkswagen, and there was no evidence that Club 24's relationship Volkswagen had been harmed in any way. Also, Mrs. Whitham had apologised immediately.
The tribunal said that Club 24 should have considered her unblemished service record and demotion would have been a better alternative to

dismissal. The Employment Tribunal said that her dismissal was unfair.

In **Smith v Trafford Housing Association [2012]** the High Court said that there was no damage to the employer's reputation. Mr. Smith was entitled to express his views as a) his Facebook page was personal; b) the comment was made outside of working hours so that no reasonable person would conclude that they were made on the trust's behalf; and c) his views were commonly held and promoted in the press, and were therefore, when viewed objectively, not offensive.

In contrast, the employment tribunal case of **Weeks v Everything Everywhere Ltd [2012],** is one where Mr. Weeks was held to have been fairly dismissed for making threats on Facebook to a colleague and describing his place of work as "Dante's Inferno", even though he did not mention the company's name. Mr. Week's colleague reported him to the employer. Mr. Weeks was unrepentant, and continued to post in the same vein on Facebook. He made comments like *"eat cake bitch"* that made the colleague feel threatened. Mr. Weeks was dismissed for bringing Everything Everywhere into disrepute.

He lost his claim for unfair dismissal because the tribunal said that the decision to dismiss was "proportionate to the seriousness of the offence or offences". The tribunal based the decision on Mr. Week's truculent approach to his employers, his refusal to stop making further derogatory references, and the threatening comments to his colleague.

In **Stephens v Halfords Plc [2010],** Halfords had a social media policy which prohibited staff from making any comments on social media that were not in the best interests of the company or that could encourage dissent. Mr. Stephens was employed as a Deputy Store Manager with Halfords. The company was contemplating redundancies and had started the collective consultation process. Mr. Stephens knew that the consultation was confidential until it was completed at which point all Halfords employees would be informed of the proposals.

Although he was on sick leave with stress Mr. Stephens attended the consultation meetings. He felt that the employee website was not a suitable forum to discuss the redundancies so he set up a Facebook page to provide a forum for employees where he posted, *"Halfords workers against working 3 out of 4 weekends"*.

Shortly after setting up the forum he realised that the Facebook page breached Halfords social media policy, so he closed down the page on the same day that he set it up. When Halfords found out, Mr. Stephens was disciplined and dismissed for breach of trust for posting confidential information on a social networking site.

The tribunal disagreed with Halfords and said that no reasonable employer could have concluded that dismissal was appropriate given that Mr. Stephens had apologised for his actions and removed the page as soon as he realised it was contrary to the Respondent's policy. There was nothing to indicate that his continuing employment was untenable.

In **Trasler v B&Q Ltd [2012],** Mr. Trasler was summarily dismissed after he posted on Facebook that B&Q is beyond a *"f****** joke"* and that he would soon be *"doing some busting".* He ended the post with LMAO (laugh my ass off). His colleague reported him to his employer.

B&Q interpreted this as he intended to do some damage to property and disciplined him for breach of their social media policy, which prohibited the making of comments which were derogatory, defamatory, rude, threatening or insulting to the company or colleagues. The comments could be read by 40 to 50 people who would be aware that they related to B & Q. The employment tribunal said that his dismissal was unfair for the following reasons;
— It was a one off posting done of the frustration of a bad day.
— There was no evidence that anyone had felt threatened by the comments.
— He had a clean disciplinary record and four years' service.
— The comments had not posed any threat to the business and the tribunal did not accept B & Q's evidence that Mr Stephens could damage company property, based on the comments made.

The tribunal said that B & Q had not proved a sufficient reason for dismissal, or that the comments had so undermined trust and confidence that Mr. Stephens could no longer be employed. The decision to dismiss was outside the band of reasonable response.

Kass v Gillies and Mackay Ltd (unreported – July 2013) here, Niall Kass was a driver for building company Gillies and Mackay Ltd. Mr. Kass was stopped by police, and fined £60 fixed penalty because his MOT was out-of-date. He posted an angry message on Facebook criticising his employers for not doing their job properly.

His message was seen by up to 100 Facebook friends and one of them was the company's business manager, Carra Marshall. She was extremely angry and annoyed and asked him to remove the post immediately. Mr. Kass had made the original posting on his iPhone but did not know how to delete it on the iPhone so he waited until after work and deleted it on his parent's desk top computer.

Meanwhile, Ms. Marshall told her father John Mackay, one of the two directors. He saw the message, was angry and decided: *"We just have to get rid of him."* Mr. Kass was disciplined and dismissed. He sued Gillies and Mackay Ltd. for unfair dismissal.

The Employment Tribunal Hearing
The tribunal said that Mr Kass had every right to be upset when, because of his employers' shortcomings, he received the fixed penalty notice. The dismissal was not proportionate to the offence since his comments were not available to the general public.

Mr Kass had not been given adequate opportunity to explain himself, and his appeal had not been carried out independently. Gillies and Mackay had overreacted since before Facebook, Mr Kass would have "vented his frustration by telling his friends and family of the incident directly or on the telephone," and this would not have been grounds for summary dismissal. The employment tribunal said that the dismissal of Niall Kass was unfair.

Mason v Huddersflied Giants Rugby League FC (unreported – July 2013) was a rugby league player who was summarily dismissed for posting photo a picture of his naked bottom on his Twitter account which had 4,200 followers. He deleted it 48 hours later but his contract was cancelled. The Judge said that his dismissal was unfair for the following reasons;

— There was clear evidence that the Huddersfield Giants wanted Mr Mason to leave the club. Two new players had been taken on and there had been attempts to transfer him. This was the main reason for dismissal and note the Twitter post.
— His actions were not a breach of contract.
— It was very unlikely that a fan seeing the tweet would assume it had been condoned by the club.

In **Young v Argos Ltd** (unreported 2011), Ms. Young "liked" a comment on Facebook that her manager was "as much use as a chocolate teapot". She commented it had been the worst of her 15 years with the company and she was glad her colleague had escaped. Argos dismissed her and she sued for unfair dismissal.
The employment tribunal said liking someone's comments and her own post was not serious enough to constitute bullying or harassment, and was

just office gossip. Ms. Young's dismissal was unfair because no reasonable employer could have concluded that her comments amounted to gross misconduct.

In **Taylor v Somerfield Stores [2007],** a video was posted on YouTube of an employee "striking" another with a plastic bag filled with other plastic bags. It was on YouTube for three days and only viewed eight times, including three times by Somerfield managers. The employee was dismissed for "gross misconduct for posting inappropriate film footage onto the YouTube website which brought the company into disrepute".

A Scottish employment tribunal said the dismissal was unfair because Mr. Taylor had apologised, there was no evidence that Somerfield's reputation had been brought into disrepute and the sanction was too harsh.

APPENDICES

Appendix 1 - Checklist

Identification

Did you use your real name or an alias? Your employer can make a disclosure request or S5 Defamation Act 2013 application to the web-site host. This would identify the computer from which a message was posted, and not necessarily the person who posted it. Check this before admitting to anything.

Policy

1. Does your employer have a social media or other relevant policy?
2. Does your employer have a disciplinary policy?
3. Was it published before or after the allegations against you?
4. Have you received training and guidance on it?
5. Do you understand it?
6. What does it say about the seriousness of the allegations against you?
7. Are you aware of the potential ramifications of inappropriate comments?
8. If there is no social media policy, get a copy of the grievance policy, and consider filing a grievance.

The post or message

1. Was the message addressed to a particular person who forwarded it?
2. Are the comments targeted against any individual?
3. How was the comment published and who had access to it? For example if it was on twitter was it re-tweeted?
4. Was it capable of being shared?

5. If it was shared, how many people saw it? Did customers or other stakeholders see it?
6. Have there been any complaints? Made by who?
7. Was the message posted to more than one person? Did it mention anything about work?
8. Was it possible to identify the people or your employer from the post?
9. If it was one email intended for one person or group of people consider the Article 8 argument.
10. Did you disclose confidential information?
11. Could there be damage to your employer's reputation?

Your job

Does the allegation impact on your ability to do your job? If it doesn't say so and explain why you believe this to be the case.

Mitigating factors

1. What are the particular circumstances that made you make that post?
2. Were you stressed?
3. Do you have a clean service record?
4. Did you remove the post as soon as you knew it was offensive?
5. Have you apologised?

Appendix 2 – Statement of defence

You MUST write your statement of defence and submit it with your evidence before the hearing. Usually the disciplinary policy will have a cut-off date when all relevant documents and responses should be received by. Make sure you stick to this date. If there are no time limits in the Disciplinary Policy, then submit it in reasonable time for the hearing.

The ACAS Code of Practice says;

— *The employee should also be given a reasonable opportunity to ask questions, present evidence and call relevant witnesses. They should also be given an opportunity to raise points about any information provided by witnesses. Where an employer or employee intends to call relevant witnesses they should give advance warning.*

1. Introduction

   Start off by stating your job title and how long you have worked for.

2. Set out your case
   Use the checklist above and the detailed guidance in this book to set out your case.

   When did the incident happen, was it at work or outside work?

   Where did the incident happen?

   Who was involved, and names of any witnesses?

   Why did the incident take place?

   If the disciplinary hearing is because of a performance matter, state whether you have had any assistance to improve. If you feel that the assistance was inadequate state so.

3. <u>Refer to the policy that you are supposed to have breached</u>

    Is the allegation a misconduct or gross misconduct? Is it mentioned in any policy?

    Was the incident actually a breach of policy? Is the policy being applied correctly?

    Is the alleged breach custom and practice in your workplace?

    Have management set out guidelines or given you training? Has the policy been explained to you?

4. <u>Go through the evidence against you – Use the checklist</u>
    Is there enough evidence for your employer to reach the conclusion that you are guilty of the alleged misconduct? Point out any gaps in the evidence.

    Explain in your statement why you believe that your employer cannot draw certain conclusions from the evidence.

    Refer to your witness statements and other evidence which supports your case.

5. <u>Other things that you can mention as part of your defence (Mitigation)</u>

    What are your good qualities? Have you won any awards at work, or have you been praised by a customer. Have you had a good appraisal? Draw your employer's attention to this.

    Your length of service and clean disciplinary record if relevant.

    Is there anything happening in your personal life or at work that made you act as you did? For example are you stressed, or overworked? Have you been ill or have problems at home? Are you being bullied at work?

Have you mentioned problems previously and nothing was done? Do you feel that this inaction led to your alleged breach?

Have other people done the same thing that you did with lesser consequences?

Is it actually your fault? Did management or anyone else make mistakes that led to your actions?

Are you in a new role or department? Are you having problems adjusting to a new way of working?

6. <u>Any other matters</u>
   Have you discovered something new whilst conducting your own investigation? Ask your employer to investigate it.

EMPLOYEE RESCUE

Employers have all the information, resources, and money. If you are don't have the same resources and are not a member of a trade union, what do you have? You have Employee Rescue. Employment Law is heavily biased in favour of the well informed. Information is your friend and that's what Employee Rescue provides.

We are a team of employment specialist professionals with qualifications, experience and comprehensive training in UK employment law, so that we can help you with your employment issues. We don't operate on a "no win, no fee" basis, or provide you with any representation. What we do is provide you with the best advice on your problem on all your employment law requirements in disputes with your employer, so that you can handle it yourself or make sure that your chosen representative is giving you the right support and information.

Employee Rescue specialists provide you with all the information and support you could possibly need to make your claim. From internal procedures, ACAS Early Conciliation, Employment Tribunal, Employment Appeal Tribunal, County Court to High Court.

Go to www.employeerescue.co.uk for more.

ABOUT THE AUTHOR

Cilinnie Ngo-Pondi (LLb.Hons) is a legal professional with over two decades experience of supporting and representing employees in the UK, New Zealand, Australia and Africa. Working with individual employees and trade unions, she has amassed a wealth of knowledge and experience of the employment problems that matter to you.

[i] The Guardian: Facebook, 10 years of social networking in numbers http://www.theguardian.com/news/datablog/2014/feb/04/facebook-in-numbers-statistics

[ii] The Independent: LinkedIn passes the 15 million user landmark in UK http://www.independent.co.uk/life-style/gadgets-and-tech/news/linkedin-passes-15-million-user-landmark-in-uk--including-five-mermaids-9186920.html

[iii] ACAS: Social media and Managing Performance

www.ingramcontent.com/pod-product-compliance
Lightning Source LLC
Chambersburg PA
CBHW070930180526
45168CB00003B/1017